William J. Seymour
& His Azusa Street Sermons
Douglas Harrolf

This edition first published in 2016 by HJ Publishing.
Copyright © 2016 HJ Publishing

All rights reserved. No part of this publication may be reproduced, distributed, or transmitted in any form or by any means, including photocopying, recording, or other electronic or mechanical methods, without the prior written permission of the publisher, except in the case of brief quotations embodied in critical reviews and certain other non-commercial uses permitted by copyright law.

For permission requests or for more information about this book visit hjpublishing.com

www.hjpublishing.com

Contents

FORWARD BY THE EDITOR 4

THE PRECIOUS ATONEMENT 6

THE WAY INTO THE HOLIEST 8

RIVER OF LIVING WATER 9

IN MONEY MATTERS 13

"BEHOLD THE BRIDEGROOM COMETH!" 18

"RECEIVE YE THE HOLY GHOST" 20

GIFTS OF THE SPIRIT 22

REBECCA; TYPE OF THE BRIDE OF CHRIST — GEN 24 24

THE BAPTISM WITH THE HOLY GHOST 29

THE MARRIAGE TIE 36

MARRIAGE BINDING FOR LIFE 37

LETTER TO ONE SEEKING THE HOLY GHOST 41

CHRIST'S MESSAGES TO THE CHURCH 44

"TO THE MARRIED" 52

SANCTIFIED ON THE CROSS 57

THE BAPTISM OF THE HOLY GHOST 59

THE HOLY GHOST AND THE BRIDE 65

Forward by the Editor

I'm not sure what I like most about William J. Seymour. There's the obvious fact that he is the person many consider to be the father of the Pentecostal Movement. That's obviously worth admiring, whether you're looking at the Pentecostal beliefs from either a theological or experiential viewpoint, or a combination of the two.

These days there are plenty of books about revivals, current and past. Outpourings are currently happening in the US, Europe, Mexico, South America, China, and Africa. Although we all long for the day when it becomes a global phenomenon, it's fair to say that there are definitely plenty of places where the Holy Spirit is moving in extraordinary ways today.

In William Seymour's case, things were very different. While he believed in the baptism of the Holy Spirit, he didn't have any first-hand experience of it. There weren't even any books on the subject.
When he first heard about the baptism in the Holy Spirit, it was at a Bible School under Charles Parham, another revivalist linked with the Topeka Revival of 1901. Due to the strict laws at the time, Seymour being black, had to take his notes from outside the classroom as there were white students in the classroom.

God doesn't see color of course, and when it came to pouring out a fresh revival of the Holy Spirit, William was the perfect vessel. Perhaps it was God's sense of humor that he wanted to unleash this blessing through a black person, forcing both colors to come together in order to receive it. It's also possible of course that aside from his color and God's sense of humor, William Seymour was also hungry enough to pray and fast until he saw this happen.

That isn't to say he wasn't met with opposition. Not only was his skin a hindrance to him, but he was physically locked out of the small church he had been asked to preach at. The rulers opposed this new message about the baptism of the Holy Spirit, especially since William himself had no personal experience of it. Faith, it seems, simply wasn't enough. So instead, he began to minister to a small prayer and Bible study group that had begun meeting at 214 North Bonnie Brae.

Brother Seymour wouldn't be the first person in the group to receive this baptism. Edward Lee, the owner of the home where the group met, was the first. Of course, this only made William Seymour hungrier for God and his persistence was rewarded with his own personal outpouring shortly after.

Following this, the group grew so much over the next few days that William Seymour was forced to preach from the porch of the house before the group eventually moved into the building at 312 Azusa Street.

The sermons within this book are those which can be directly attributed to William Seymour. My thanks and the dedication of this book goes to Clara Lum, Florence Crawford, and Glen A. Cook, all of whom helped to record Brother Seymour's Azusa Street Sermons.

Douglas Harrolf

The Precious Atonement

Children of God, partakers of the precious atonement, let us study and see what there is in it for us.

First. Through the atonement we receive forgiveness of sins.
Second. We receive sanctification through the blood of Jesus.

"Wherefore Jesus also that he might sanctify the people with his own blood, suffered without the gate." Sanctified from all original sin, we become sons of God. "For both he that sanctifieth and they who are sanctified are all of one: for which cause he is not ashamed to call them brethren." Heb. 2:11. (It seems that Jesus would be ashamed to call them brethren, if they were not sanctified.) Then you will not be ashamed to tell men and demons that you are sanctified, and are living a pure and holy life free from sin, a life that gives you power over the world, the flesh, and the devil. The devil does not like that kind of testimony. Through this precious atonement, we have freedom from all sin, though we are living in this old world, we are permitted to sit in heavenly places in Christ Jesus.

Third. Healing of our bodies. Sickness and disease are destroyed through the precious atonement of Jesus. O how we ought to honor the stripes of Jesus, for "with his stripes we are healed." How we ought to honor that precious body which the Father sanctified and sent into the world, not simply set apart, but really sanctified, soul, body and spirit, free from sickness, disease and everything of the devil. A body that knew no sin and disease was given for these imperfect bodies of ours. Not only is the atonement for the sanctification of our souls, but for the sanctification of our bodies from inherited disease. It matters not what has been in the blood.

Every drop of blood we received from our mother is impure. Sickness is born in a child just as original sin is born in the child. He was manifested to destroy the works of the devil. Every sickness is of the devil.

Man in the Garden of Eden was pure and happy and knew no sickness till that unholy visitor came into the garden, then his whole system was poisoned and it has been flowing in the blood of all the human family down the ages till God spoke to his people and said, "I am the Lord that healeth thee." The children of Israel practiced divine healing.

David, after being healed of rheumatism, (perhaps contracted in the caves where he hid himself from his pursuers,) testified saying, "Bless the Lord, O my soul, and all that is within me bless his holy name, who forgiveth all thine iniquities, who healeth all thy diseases." David knew what it was to be healed. Healing continued with God's people till Solomon's heart was turned away by strange wives, and he brought in the black arts and mediums, and they went whoring after familiar spirits. God had been their healer, but after they lost the Spirit, they turned to the arm of flesh to find something to heal their diseases.

Thank God, we have a living Christ among us to heal our diseases. He will heal every case. The prophet had said, "With his stripes we are healed," and it was fulfilled when Jesus came. Also "He hath borne our griefs," (which means sickness, as translators tell us.) Now if Jesus bore our sicknesses, why should we bear them? So we get full salvation through the atonement of Jesus.

Fourth. And we get the baptism with the Holy Ghost and fire upon the sanctified life. We get Christ enthroned and crowned in our hearts. Let us lift up Christ to the world in all His fullness, not only in healing and salvation from all sin, but in His power to speak all the languages of the world. We need the triune God to enable us to do this.

We that are the messengers of this precious atonement ought to preach all of it, justification, sanctification, healing, the baptism with the Holy Ghost, and signs following. "How shall we escape if we neglect so great salvation?" God is now confirming His word by granting signs and wonders to follow the preaching of the full gospel in Los Angeles.

The Way into the Holiest

A sinner comes to the Lord all wrapped up in sin and darkness. He cannot make any consecration because he is dead. The life has to be put into us before we can present any life to the Lord. He must get justified by faith. There is a Lamb without spot and blemish slain before God for him, and when he repents toward God for his sins, the Lord has mercy on him for Christ's sake, and puts eternal life in his soul, pardoning him of his sins, washing away his guilty pollution, and he stands before God justified as if he had never sinned.

Then there remains that old original sin in him for which he is not responsible till he has the light. He hears that "Jesus, that He might sanctify the people with His own blood, suffered without the gate," and he comes to be sanctified. There is Jesus, the Lamb without blemish, on the altar. Jesus takes that soul that has eternal life in it and presents it to God for thorough purging and cleansing from all original and Adamic sin. And Jesus, the Son of God, cleanses him from all sin, and he is made every whit whole, sanctified and holy.

Now he is on the altar ready for the fire of God to fall, which is the baptism with the Holy Ghost. It is a free gift upon the sanctified, cleansed heart. The fire remains there continually burning in the holiness of God. Why? Because he is sanctified and holy and on the altar continually. He stays there and the great Shekina of glory is continually burning and filling with heavenly light.

River of Living Water

In the 4th chapter of John, the words come, "Jesus answered and said unto her, If thou knewest the gift of God and who it is that saith to thee Give me to drink, thou wouldest have asked of Him and He would have given the living water." Praise God for the living waters today that flow freely, for it comes from God to every hungry and thirsty heart. Jesus said, "He that believeth on me, as the Scripture hath said, out of his inmost being shall flow rivers of living waters." Then we are able to go in the mighty name of Jesus to the ends of the earth and water dry places, deserts and solitary places, until these parched, sad, lonely hearts are made to rejoice in the God of their salvation. We want the rivers today. Hallelujah! Glory to God in the highest!

In Jesus Christ we get forgiveness of sin, and we get sanctification of our spirit, soul, and body, and upon that we get the gift of the Holy Ghost that Jesus promised to His disciples, the promise of the Father. All this we get through the atonement. Hallelujah!

The prophet said that he had borne our griefs and carried our sorrows. He was wounded for our transgressions, bruised for our iniquities, the chastisement of our peace was upon Him and with His stripes we are healed. So we get healing, health, salvation, joy, life—everything in Jesus. Glory to God!

There are many wells today, but they are dry. There are many hungry souls today that are empty. But let us come to Jesus and take Him at His word and we will find wells of salvation, and be able to draw waters out of the well of salvation, for Jesus is that well.

At this time Jesus was weary from a long journey, and He sat on the well in Samaria, and a woman came to draw water. He asked her for a drink. She answered, "How is it that thou being a Jew askest drink of me who am a woman of Samaria, for the Jews have no dealings with the Samaritans?" Jesus said, "If thou knewest the gift of God, and who it is that saith to thee, give me to drink, thou wouldst have asked of him and he would have given thee living water."

O, how sweet it was to see Jesus, the Lamb of God that takes away the sin of the world, that great sacrifice that God had given to a lost, dying, and benighted world, sitting on the well and talking with the woman; so gentle, so meek, and so kind that it gave her an appetite to talk further with Him, until He got into her secret and uncovered her life.

Then she was pricked in heart, confessed her sins and received pardon, cleansing from fornication and adultery, was washed from stain and guilt of sin and was made a child of God, and above all, received the well of salvation in her heart. It was so sweet and joyful and good. Her heart was so filled with love that she felt she could take in a whole lost world. So she ran away with a well of salvation and left the old water pot on the well. How true it is in this day, when we get the baptism with the Holy Spirit, we have something to tell, and it is that the blood of Jesus Christ cleanseth from all sin. The baptism with the Holy Ghost gives us power to testify to a risen, resurrected Savior. Our affections are in Jesus Christ, the Lamb of God that takes away the sin of the world. How I worship Him today! How I praise Him for the all-cleansing blood!

Jesus' promises are true and sure. The woman said to Him, after He had uncovered her secret, "Sir, I perceive that Thou art a prophet." Yes, He was a prophet. He was that great prophet that Moses said the Lord would raise up. He is here today. Will we be taught of that prophet? Will we hear Him? Let us accept Him in all His fullness. He said, "He that believeth on me, the works that I do shall he do also, and greater works that these shall ye do, because I go unto my Father."

These disciples to whom He was speaking, had been saved, sanctified, anointed with the Holy Spirit, their hearts had been opened to understand the Scriptures, and yet Jesus said, "Tarry ye, in the city of Jerusalem, until ye be endued with power from on high." "John truly baptized with water, but ye shall be baptized with the Holy Ghost not many days hence." So the same commission comes to us. We find that they obeyed His commission and were all filled with the Holy Ghost on the day of Pentecost, and Peter standing up, said, "This is that which was spoken by the prophet Joel." Dear loved ones, we preach the same sermon. "This is that which was spoken by the prophet Joel, and it shall come to pass in the last days, saith God, I will pour out of my Spirit upon all flesh, and your sons and your daughters shall prophesy, and your young men shall see visions, and your old men shall dream dreams; and on my servants and on my handmaidens I will pour out in those days of my Spirit, and they shall prophesy. The promise is unto you, and to your children, and to all that are afar off, even as many as the Lord our God shall call." That means until now and to last until Jesus comes.

There are so many people today like the woman. They are controlled by the fathers. Our salvation is not in some father or human instrument. It is sad to see people so blinded, worshiping the creature more than the Creator. Listen to what the woman said, "Our Fathers worshipped in this mountain, and ye say that in Jerusalem is the place where men ought to worship." So many people today are worshipping in the mountains, big churches, stone and frame buildings. But Jesus teaches that salvation is not in these stone structures—not in the mountains—not in the hills, but in God. For God is a Spirit. Jesus said unto her, "Woman, believe Me, the hour cometh and now is, when ye shall neither in this mountain nor yet at Jerusalem worship the Father." So many people today are controlled by men. Their salvation reaches out no further than the boundary line of human creeds, but praise God for freedom in the Spirit. There are depths and heights and breadths that we can reach through the power of the blessed Spirit. "Eye hath not seen, nor ear heard, neither have entered into the heart of man the things that God hath prepared for them that love him.

The Jews were the religious leaders at this time, and people had no more light upon salvation than the Jews gave them. The Jews were God's chosen people to evangelize the world. He had entrusted them to give all nations the true knowledge of God, but they went into traditions and doctrines of men, and were blinded and in the dark.

Jesus came as the light of the world, and He is that light. "If we walk in the light as he is in the light, we have fellowship one with another, and the blood of Jesus Christ his Son cleanseth us from all sin." Let us honor the Spirit, for Jesus has sent Him to teach and lead us into all truth.

Above all, let us honor the blood of Jesus Christ every moment of our lives, and we will be sweet in our souls. We will be able to talk of this common salvation to everyone that we meet. God will let His anointing rest upon us in telling them of this precious truth. This truth belongs to God. We have no right to tax anyone for the truth, because God has entrusted us with it to tell it. Freely we receive, freely we give. So the Gospel is to be preached freely, and God will bless it and spread it Himself, and we have experienced that He does, We have found Him true to His promise all the way. We have tried Him and proved Him.

His promises are sure.

In Money Matters

There have been teachers who have told all the people to sell out, and many of them have gone into fanaticism. We let the Spirit lead people and tell them what they ought to give. When they get filled with the Spirit, their pocket books are converted and God makes them stewards and if He says, "Sell out," they will do so. But sometimes they have families. God does not tell you to forsake your family. He says if you do not provide for your own you are worse than an infidel. Some are not called to go out and teach. We find some who have no wisdom nor faith, and the devil takes them to disgrace the work. Under false teaching, children have been left to go half naked, women have left their husbands, and husbands leave their wives to wash and scrub, and the Bible says that is worse than infidelity. Then they will go and borrow and cannot pay back. That person ought to go to work. The Bible says, "Let him labor, working with his hands the thing which is good, that he may have to give to him that needeth."

He sent those that were called out to preach the Gospel, to "take no thought what ye shall eat or drink." Get down and pray. Make your wants known unto God and He will send it in.

God does not expect all to sell out for He says in 1 Cor. 16:1, "Now concerning the collection for the saints, upon the first day of the week, let everyone of you lay by him in store, as God hath prospered him." It does not mean for you to have great real estate and money banked up while your brothers and sisters are suffering. He means for you to turn loose because all that money is soon going to be thrown to the moles and bats. So it is better to spread the Gospel and get stars in your crown than to be holding it. But for us to go and tell you to do it, pick out somebody that has money and read the Word to them, would not be the Spirit of the Lord. The Spirit will tell you what to do. He makes you do it. When He wakes you up at night and tells you what to do you cannot sleep till you obey. He says everyone shall be taught of God from the least to the greatest. God wants a free giver.

Ananias wanted to have a reputation that he sold out like the rest, so he plotted that he should give a portion and say he had sold out for the Lord. But the Holy Ghost told Peter that Ananias had told a lie. Peter told him the property was his. The Lord allows you to be the steward over it. The property was his and the sin was in lying to the Holy Ghost. It is right for you to have property, but if the Lord says, take $200 or $500 or $1,000 and distribute here or there, you do it.

We must know our calling. We can work when baptized with the Holy Ghost. Some think they have got to preach. Well, we do preach in testifying. Some think they must go out because they have the tongues but those are good for Los Angeles or anywhere else. The Lord will lead you by His small voice.

Counterfeits

God has told us in His precious word that we should know a tree by its fruit. Wherever we find the real, we find the counterfeit also. But praise God for the real. We find in the time of Peter, when men and women were receiving the power of the Holy Ghost, the counterfeit appeared in Ananias and Sapphira. But God's power was mightier than all the forces of hell, so their sin found them out. Be careful, dear loved ones, for your sin will surely find you out. "But if we walk in the light as He is in the light, we have fellowship one with another and the blood of Jesus Christ his Son cleanseth us from all sin."

In our meetings, we have had people to come and claim that they had received the baptism with the Holy Spirit, but when they were put to the test by the Holy Spirit, they were found wanting. So they got down and got saved and sanctified and baptized with the Holy Spirit and spoke in tongues by the Holy Spirit. And again people have imitated the gift of tongues, but how quickly the Holy Spirit would reveal to every one of the true children that had the Pentecostal baptism, and put a heavy rebuke upon the counterfeit, in tongues, until the counterfeits were silenced and condemned. God's promises are true and sure.

People are trying to imitate the work of the Holy Ghost these days, just as they did when the Lord sent Moses to Pharaoh in Ex. 7:8, and gave him a miracle or sign to show before Pharaoh, that when Aaron should cast his rod before Pharaoh, it should become a serpent. So when Pharaoh saw that Aaron's rod had become a serpent, he called for his wise men and the counterfeit sorcerers and magicians of Egypt. They also did in like manner with their enchantments, for they cast down every man his rod, and they became serpents, but Aaron's rod swallowed up their rods. So the power of the Holy Ghost in God's people today condemns and swallows up the counterfeit. It digs up and exposes all the power of Satan—Christian Science, Theosophy, and Spiritualism—all are uncovered before the Son of God. Glory to God.

Spiritualists have come to our meetings and had the demons cast out of them and have been saved and sanctified. Christian Scientists have come to the meetings and had the Christian Science demons cast out of them and have accepted the blood. Every plant that my heavenly Father hath not planted shall be rooted up.

People have come to this place full of demons and God has cast them out, and they have gone out crying with loud voices. Then when all the demons were cast out, they got saved, sanctified, and baptized with the Holy Ghost, clothed in their right minds and filled with glory and power.

Dear loved ones; it is not by might nor by power but by my Spirit, saith the Lord. "Tarry ye in the city of Jerusalem, until ye be endued with power from on high. John truly baptized with water, but ye shall be baptized with the Holy Ghost not many days hence." These were Jesus' departing words. May you tarry until you receive your personal Pentecost. Amen.

"Then shall the kingdom of heaven be likened unto ten virgins, which took their lamps, and went forth to meet the bridegroom. And five of them were wise and five were foolish. They that were foolish took their lamps and took no oil with them; but the wise took oil in their vessels with their lamps.

"While the bridegroom tarried, they all slumbered and slept. And at midnight, there was a cry made, Behold the bridegroom: go ye out to meet him.

"Then all those virgins arose and trimmed their lamps. And the foolish said unto the wise, Give us of your oil, for our lamps are gone out. (R.V. Going Out.) But the wise answered saying, Not so; lest there be not enough for us and you; but go ye rather to them that sell, and buy for yourselves.

"And while they went to buy the bridegroom came; and they that were ready went in with him to the marriage; and the door was shut. Afterward came also the other virgins saying, Lord, Lord, open to us. But he answered and said, Verily I say unto you, I know you not.

"Watch therefore, for ye know neither the day nor the hour wherein the Son of Man cometh." Matt. 25:1-13.

You know virgin in the scripture is a type of purity. Christ is speaking in this parable about the church and its condition at His coming. Many precious souls today are not looking for the return of their Lord, and they will be found in the same condition as the five foolish virgins.

They started out to meet the bridegroom, and had some oil in their lamps but none in their vessels with their lamps. So when the cry was made to go forth, they were found wanting in oil, which is the real type of the Holy Ghost. Many of God's children are cleansed from sin and yet fight against getting more oil. They think they have enough. They have some of God's love in their souls, but they have not the double portion of it. The thing they need is oil in their vessels with their lamps.

It is just as plain as can be.

Dearly beloved, the Scripture says, "Blessed are they which are called to the marriage supper of the Lamb." Rev. 19:9. So they are blessed that have the call. Those that will be permitted to enter in are those who are justified, sanctified, and baptized with the Holy Ghost—sealed unto the day of redemption. O may God stir up His waiting bride everywhere to get oil in their vessels with their lamps that they may enter into the marriage supper. The Holy Ghost is sifting out a people that are getting on the robes of righteousness and the seal in their foreheads. The angel is holding the winds now till all the children of God are sealed in their foreheads with the Father's name. Then the wrath of God is going to be poured out.

"Behold the Bridegroom Cometh!"

O the time is very near. All the testimonies of His coming that have been going on for months are a witness that He is coming soon. But when the trumpet sounds, it will be too late to prepare. Those that are not ready at the rapture will be left to go through the awful tribulation that is coming upon the earth.

The wise virgins will be at the marriage supper and spend the time of the great tribulation with the Lord Jesus. They will have glorified bodies. For we which remain unto the coming of the Lord will be changed in the twinkling of an eye.

Many precious souls believe today that in sanctification they have it all, that they have already the baptism with the Holy Ghost or enduement of power; but in that day, they will find they are mistaken. They say, Away with this third work. What is the difference, dear ones, if it takes 300 works? We want to be ready to meet the bridegroom. The foolish virgins said to the wise, "Give us of your oil." This thing is going to happen. Many that are saying they have enough and are opposing, will find their lamps going out and ask the prayers of God's people. God is warning you through His servants and handmaidens to get ready; but many are going to come back to get the oil from others. Dear ones, we cannot get more than enough for ourselves. You can grasp the saints' hands but you cannot squeeze any oil out. You have to get the vessel filled for yourself. Many are going to be marrying and giving in marriage, buying and selling, and the cares of this world are going to get in the way. Above all, we want to get the oil, the Holy Ghost. Every Christian must be baptized with the Holy Ghost for himself. Many poor souls in that day will be awfully disappointed. May we seek Him today, the baptism with the Holy Ghost and fire. Now is the time to buy the oil; that is by tarrying at the feet of the Lord Jesus and receiving the baptism with the Holy Spirit.

It seems that people will be able to buy oil during the rapture. It seems that the Spirit will still be here on earth and that they could get it, but it will be too late for the marriage supper. So the Lord warns us to be ready, for we know not the day nor the hour.

Those that get left in the rapture and still prove faithful to God and do not receive the mark of the beast, though they will have to suffer martyrdom, will be raised to reign with Christ. Antichrist will reign during the tribulation and everything will be controlled by him and by the false prophet, when they have succeeded in uniting the whole world in acknowledging the antichrist. Those that acknowledge him will be permitted to buy and sell, but those that stand faithful to the Lord Jesus and testify to the Blood will be killed for the word of their testimony. But by proving faithful to death, they will be raised during the millennium and reign with Christ. But we that are caught up to the marriage supper of the Lamb will escape the plagues that are coming on the earth.

May God fit everyone of us for the coming of the Lord, that we may come back with him on white horses and help Him to execute judgment on the earth and make way for the millennial kingdom, when He shall reign from shore to shore, and righteousness shall cover the earth as waters cover the sea.

That is the time that Enoch prophesied of, "Behold the Lord cometh with ten thousand of His saints," Jude 14. "Then shall the Lord go forth and fight against these nations, as when He fought in the day of battle. And His feet shall stand in that day upon the Mount of Olives," Zec. 14:3, 4. The mountain shall be parted in two. Then shall the antichrist and the false prophet be cast into the lake of fire and brimstone and Satan shall be bound a thousand years. Rev. 19:20 and 20:2.

We shall be priests and kings unto God, reigning with Him a thousand years in a jubilee of peace. Our Christ will be King of kings and Lord of lords over the whole earth. We shall reign with Him over unglorified humanity. Some will be appointed over ten cities and some over two, and the twelve apostles will be over the twelve tribes of Israel. "To him that overcometh will I grant to sit with me in my throne, even as I also overcame and am set down with my Father in His throne." Rev. 3:21, 22.

"Receive Ye the Holy Ghost"

1.—The first step in seeking the baptism with the Holy Ghost, is to have a clear knowledge of the new birth in our souls, which is the first work of grace and brings everlasting life to our souls. "Therefore being justified by faith, we have peace with God." Every one of us that repents of our sins and turns to the Lord Jesus with faith in Him, receives forgiveness of sins. Justification and regeneration are simultaneous. The pardoned sinner becomes a child of God in justification.

2.—The next step for us is to have a clear knowledge, by the Holy Spirit, of the second work of grace wrought in our hearts by the power of the Blood and the Holy Ghost. Heb. 10:14,15, "For by one offering, He hath perfected forever them that are sanctified, whereof the Holy Ghost also is a witness to us." The Scripture also teaches (Heb. 2:11), "For both He that sanctifieth and they who are sanctified are all of one; for which cause He is not ashamed to call them brethren." So we have Christ crowned and enthroned in our hearts, the tree of life. We have the brooks and streams of salvation flowing in our souls, but praise God, we can have the rivers. For the Lord Jesus says, "He that believeth on me, as the Scripture hath said, out of his innermost being shall flow rivers of living water. This spake He of the Spirit, for the Holy Ghost was not yet given." But, praise our God, He is now given and being poured out upon all flesh. All races, nations, and tongues are receiving the baptism with the Holy Ghost and fire, according to the prophecy of Joel.

3.—When we have a clear knowledge of justification and sanctification, through the precious Blood of Jesus Christ in our hearts, then we can be a recipient of the baptism with the Holy Ghost. Many people today are sanctified, cleansed from all sin, and perfectly consecrated to God, but they have never obeyed the Lord according to Acts 1:4, 5, 8 and Luke 24:39, for their real personal Pentecost, the enduement of power for service and work and for sealing unto the day of redemption. The baptism with the Holy Ghost is a free gift without repentance, upon the sanctified, cleansed vessel. II Cor.1:21-22, "Now He which establisheth us with you in Christ, and hath anointed us, is God, who hath also sealed us, and given the earnest of the Spirit in our hearts."

Praise our God for the sealing of the Holy Spirit unto the day of redemption.

Dearly beloved, the only people that will meet our Lord and Savior Jesus Christ and go with Him into the marriage supper of the Lamb, are the wise virgins-not only saved and sanctified, with pure and clean hearts, but having the baptism with the Holy Ghost. The others we find will not be prepared. They have some oil in their lamps but they have not the double portion of His Holy Spirit.

The disciples were filled with the unction of the Holy Spirit before Pentecost that sustained them until they received the Holy Ghost baptism. Many people today are filled with joy and gladness, but they are far from the enduement of power. Sanctification brings rest and sweetness and quietness to our souls, for we are one with the Lord Jesus and are able to obey His precious Word, that "Man shall not live by bread alone, but by every word that proceedeth out of the mouth of God," and we are feeding upon Christ.

But let us wait for the promise of the Father upon our souls, according to Jesus' Word, "John truly baptized with water, but ye shall be baptized with the Holy Ghost not many days hence. Ye shall receive power after that the Holy Ghost is come upon you; and ye shall be witnesses unto me, both in Jerusalem and in all Judea, and in Samaria, and unto the uttermost part of the earth." Acts 1:1, 5, 8.

Glory! Glory! Hallelujah! O worship, get down on your knees and ask the Holy Ghost to come in, and you will find Him right at your heart's door, and He will come in. Prove Him now. Amen.—W.J.S.

Gifts of the Spirit

"Now concerning spiritual gifts brethren, I would not have you ignorant."

Paul was speaking to the Corinthian Church at this time. They were like Christ's people everywhere today. Many of His people do not know their privileges in this blessed Gospel. The Gospel of Christ is the power of God unto salvation to everyone that believeth. And in order that we might know His power, we must forever abide in the Word of God that we may have the precious fruits of the Spirit, and not only the fruits but the precious gifts that Father has for His little ones.

Dearly beloved, may we search the Scriptures and see for ourselves whether we are measuring up to every word that proceedeth out of the mouth of God. If we will remain in the Scriptures and follow the blessed Holy Spirit all the way, we will be able to measure up to the Word of God in all of its fullness. Paul prayed in Eph. 3:16, "That He would grant you, according to the riches of His glory, to be strengthened with might by His Spirit in the inner man; that Christ may dwell in your hearts by faith; that ye being rooted and grounded in love, may be able to comprehend with all saints, what is the breadth, and length, and depth, and height, and to know the love of Christ which passeth knowledge; that ye might be filled with all the fullness of God. Now unto Him that is able to do exceeding abundantly above all that we ask or think, according to the power that worketh in us."

Many people say today that tongues are the least gift of any that the Lord can give, and they do not need it, and ask What good is it to us? But by careful study of the Word, we see in the 14th of Corinthians, Paul telling the church to "follow after charity and desire spiritual gifts." Charity means Divine love: without which we will never be able to enter heaven. Gifts all will fail, but Divine love will last through all eternity. And right in the same verse he says, "Desire spiritual gifts, but rather that ye may prophesy," that is to say, preach in your own tongue, which will build up the saints and the church.

But he says in the next verse, "For he that speaketh in an unknown tongue, speaketh not unto men, but unto God, for no man understandeth him, howbeit in the Spirit, he speaketh mysteries, (R.V., hidden truth.) But he that prophesieth speaketh unto man to edification, exhortation and comfort." He that prophesies in his own tongue edifies the church; but he that speaks in unknown tongues edifies himself. His spirit is being edified, while the church is not edified, because they do not understand what he says unless the Lord gives somebody the interpretation of the tongue.

Here is where many stumble that have not this blessed gift to use in the Spirit. They say, What good is it when you do not know what you are talking about?

Praise God, every gift He gives is a good gift. It is very blessed, for when the Lord gets ready, He can speak in any language He chooses to speak. You ask, "Is not prophecy the best gift?" Prophecy is the best gift to the church, for it builds up the saints and edifies them and exalts them to higher things in the Lord Jesus. If a brother or sister is speaking in tongues and cannot speak any English, but preaches altogether in tongues and has no interpretation, they are less than he that prophesies, but if they interpret they are just as great.

May God help all of His precious people to read the 14th of 1 Cor., and give them the real interpretation of the Word. May we all use our gift to the glory of God and not worship the gift. The Lord gives us power to use it to His own glory and honor.

Many times, when we were receiving this blessed Pentecost, we all used to break out in tongues; but we have learned to be quieter with the gift. Often when God sends a blessed wave upon us, we all may speak in tongues for awhile, but we will not keep it up while preaching service is going on, for we want to be obedient to the Word, that everything may be done decently and in order and without confusion. Amen.

Rebecca; Type of the Bride of Christ — Gen 24

"I pray thee is there room in thy father's house for us to lodge in?" These words were spoken by Eliezer, Abraham's eldest servant and steward of his house, to Rebecca when he had found her at the well in answer to his prayer. Eliezer (meaning "God's Helper") is a type of the Holy Spirit, and Isaac is a type of Christ. Now as Eliezer was seeking a bride for Isaac, the son of Abraham, so the Holy Spirit today is seeking a bride for the Lord Jesus, God's only begotten Son.

Eliezer was sent to Abraham's country and to his kindred to take a wife for Isaac. So God our Father has sent the Holy Spirit from the glory land down into this world, and He, the Spirit of truth, is convicting the world of sin, righteousness, and judgment, and is selecting out of the body of Christ His bride. He is seeking among His kindred, the sanctified, and Jesus is baptizing them with the Holy Ghost and fire, preparing them for the great marriage supper of the Lamb. Praise our God! Eliezer was under oath not to select the bride from the Canaanites but from Abraham's kindred. So God is not selecting a bride for Christ among the sinners, for a sinner must first get saved and sanctified before he can be one with the Lord Jesus. Heb. 2:11 says, "For both He that sanctifieth and they who are sanctified are all of one, for which cause He is not ashamed to call them brethren." So He is seeking a bride among His brethren, the sanctified.

"Christ so loved the church that He gave Himself for it; that He might sanctify and cleanse it with the washing of water by the Word; that He might present it unto Himself a glorious church, not having spot or wrinkle or any such thing; but that it should be holy and without blemish." Eph. 5:25-27. So Jesus today is selecting a sanctified people, baptizing them with the Holy Ghost and fire to greet Him at His coming. Rebecca was a virgin, the type of a sanctified soul. So the Holy Ghost today is standing at the heart of every pure virgin (sanctified soul) pleading, "I pray thee is there room in thy heart that I may come in and lodge?" O beloved, we see many of the sanctified people today rejecting the Holy Spirit, just as people rejected Christ when He was on earth here. It seems there is no room in their hearts for the baptism with the Holy Ghost and fire. May God help them to open their eyes and see that the time draweth nigh for His coming. O may Christ's waiting bride wake up and let the Holy Ghost come in.

Rebecca was a type of the wise virgins. When Eliezer met her at the well and asked her to let him drink a little water from her pitcher, O how sweet and ready she was. She answered and said, "Drink, my Lord." And she hastened and let down her pitcher upon her hand and gave him drink, and it pleased him. The Spirit is a person. He can be pleased, He can be quenched, and He can be insulted, as we find Ananias insulted Him. We please Him when we accept the words of Jesus. Then Jesus sends the Holy Spirit to witness in our hearts.

When Rebecca had done giving him drink, she said, "I will also draw water for thy camels." Christ's bride must do everything without murmuring. O how sweet it is when we have the mighty Spirit in our hearts; we are ready for service; we are ready for watering the whole entire world with the precious well of salvation in our heart. Beloved, when the Holy Ghost comes, He brings the well of salvation and rivers of living water.

"And it came to pass, as the camels had done drinking, that the man took a gold earring of half a shekel weight and two bracelets for her hands of ten shekels weight of gold." Praise God. This is what our beloved sanctified people receive when they receive the witness of the anointing of the Holy Ghost upon their hearts, as when Jesus breathed upon the disciples before Pentecost in the upper room, where He said, "Receive ye the Holy Ghost." The disciples had the witness in their hearts that very moment that "both He that sanctifieth and they who are sanctified are all of one." For He had opened the Scriptures to them, (Lu. 24:32) and their understanding was opened, (Lu. 24:31) "And their eyes were opened and they knew Him." So with us, when we receive sanctification and the witness of the Spirit in our hearts to our sanctification, the Scriptures are opened to us, we understand them, and our eyes are anointed. We see a picture of it in Rebecca. When she had received Eliezer and let him drink out of her pitcher and had watered the camels, he gave her the earrings and bracelets of gold.

O beloved may we let the Holy Ghost sup out of our heart pitcher, for the Lord says, "Behold, I stand at the door and knock; if any man hear My voice and open the door, I will come in and sup with him and he with Me."
And when He comes in, He opens His precious treasures to us, bracelets and earrings, great weights of gold. O how blessed it is when the precious Spirit enters into our hearts like Eliezer. He tells us the great wealth of our Father and of our Christ, for He opens up our understanding, and enlightens our minds. His continual conversation is about the Father and Jesus. Eliezer was the very type of the Holy Spirit who takes the things of Christ and shows them unto us, for He told Rebecca of the wealth of Abraham and Isaac, giving her jewels. And she wore them, showing that she was the espoused of Isaac. Hallelujah! Jesus breathed the Holy Ghost on His disciples and said, "Whose soever sins ye remit, they are remitted unto them; and whose soever sins ye retain, they are retained." Thus they had the witness in their hearts that they were candidates for the baptism with the Holy Ghost and fire. He commanded them, "Tarry ye in the city of Jerusalem, until ye endued with power from on high." Praise our God!

"I pray thee is there room in thy father's house for us to lodge in?" Beloved, is there room in your heart that God's blessed Spirit can come and lodge in? Rebecca was a wise virgin. She met Eliezer at the well and received the bracelets and earrings; but she did not receive them until she had allowed him to drink out of her pitcher and had watered the camels. Many others stood by, no doubt; but they did not do any watering of the camels. O may all of Christ's waiting bride be filled with the rivers of living water that they may water the thirsty, parched hearts with the rivers of salvation.

Rebecca wore her jewels. She did not put them aside or into her pocket, for we read that Laban saw them on his sister's hands. When we have received the abiding anointing in our hearts, someone can always see it shining forth upon our faces. Praise God!

When Eliezer had fed the camels and had come into the house, and when meat was set before him, he said, "I will not eat until I have told mine errand." O beloved, we should be so zealous about the bride of Christ that nothing will be able to turn us aside. We find the first overthrow in the human soul was through the appetite; and when the Holy Ghost sends us on His mission, may we not be satisfied until we have told it, and of His coming back to earth again.
Then he told his mission how that Abraham had sent him to his kindred to take a wife for his son, and he said, "And now if ye will deal kindly and truly with my master, tell me, and if not, tell me." They said, "The thing proceedeth from the Lord" and gave Rebecca to be his master's wife. When people are living under the guidance of God's Holy Spirit, it does not take them very long to hear the voice of God, and they are willing to obey. Praise God! Then Eliezer ate and tarried with them that night, because he had received the desire of his master's heart and his heart.

But on the morrow, her brother and mother said, "Let the damsel abide with us a few days, at least ten days." But he said, "Hinder me not." It is best, when we hear the words of God and the Spirit is upon us, to receive now the baptism with the Holy Spirit, instead of waiting two or three days and meeting friends and meeting the devil, who will try to persuade us out of it. If Rebecca had remained, perhaps her friends might have talked her out of going with Eliezer over the plains away off to that distant land to her husband Isaac.

Eliezer said, "Hinder me not." O may we do nothing to hinder the entrance of the baptism with the Holy Ghost. We should see that everything is out of the way and nothing to stand between us and this glorious blessing. Then they called Rebecca and said to her, "Wilt thou go with this man?" And she said, "I will go." To receive the baptism with the Holy Ghost, we must forsake all and follow Jesus all the way.

For the Lord Jesus says, "For this cause shall a man leave his father and mother, and cleave to his wife." So we that are Christ's bride must forsake all and cleave to Christ, as Rebecca left father and mother, brother and sister, and rode on the camel to meet Isaac.

"And Isaac went out to meditate in the fields at eventide; and he lifted up his eyes and saw, and behold the camels were coming. And Rebecca lifted up her eyes, and when she saw Isaac, she lighted off the camel" to meet him. Now we are living in the eventide of this dispensation, when the Holy Spirit is leading us, Christ's bride, to meet Him in the clouds.

The Baptism with the Holy Ghost

Dear one in Christ who are seeking the baptism with the Holy Ghost; do not seek for tongues but for the promise of the Father, and pray for the baptism with the Holy Ghost, and God will throw in the tongues according to Acts 2:4.

We read in Acts 1:4,5, "And being assembled together with them, commanded them that they should not depart from Jerusalem, but wait for the promise of the Father, which, saith He, ye have heard of me. For John truly baptized with water; but ye shall be baptized with the Holy Ghost not many days hence."

This promise of the Father was preached unto the disciples by John the Baptist. And Jesus reminded the disciples about this baptism that John had preached to them in life. In England we find the same thing. Math. 3:11. John, after warning the Jews and Pharisees against sin and hypocrisy, preached the doctrine of the baptism with the Holy Ghost. He said first, "Bring forth therefore, fruits meet for repentance." God is sending out His precious ministers to preach repentance to the people and turn them from their sins and cause them to make restitution according to their ability, and to have faith in the Lord Jesus Christ and be saved. Glory to God!

And then they must get sanctified through the precious Blood of Jesus Christ, for He says in John 17:15-19, "I pray not that Thou shouldst take them out of the world, but that thou shouldst keep them from the evil. They are not of the world, even as I am not of the world. Sanctify them through Thy truth; Thy Word is truth. As Thou hast sent Me into the world, even so have I also sent them into the world. And for their sakes I sanctify Myself, that they also might be sanctified through the truth." God wants His people to be sanctified, because He says again in Heb. 13:12, "Wherefore Jesus also that He might sanctify the people with His own Blood, suffered without the gate. Let us go forth therefore unto Him without the camp, bearing His reproach."

Then Jesus taught the disciples to tarry at Jerusalem. They obeyed Him and waited for the promise of the Father. "And when the day of Pentecost was fully come, they were all with one accord in one place. And suddenly there came a sound from heaven as of a rushing, mighty wind, and it filled all the house where they were sitting. And there appeared unto them cloven tongues like as of fire, and it sat upon each of them. And they were all filled with the Holy Ghost, and began to speak with other tongues, as the Spirit gave them utterance." Acts 2:1-4.
Wind is always typical of the Spirit or of life. "And it filled all the house where they were sitting." The rivers of salvation had come and had filled the whole place, and they all were immersed or baptized in the Holy Spirit. Praise God!

"And there appeared unto them cloven tongues like as of fire." Beloved, when we receive the baptism with the Holy Ghost and fire, we surely will speak in tongues as the Spirit gives utterance. We are not seeking for tongues, but we are seeking the baptism with the Holy Ghost and fire. And when we receive it, we shall be so filled with the Holy Ghost, that He Himself will speak in the power of the Spirit.

"And they were all filled with the Holy Ghost, and began to speak with other tongues, as the Spirit gave them utterance." Now, beloved, do not be too concerned about your speaking in tongues, but let the Holy Ghost give you utterance, and it will come just as freely as the air we breathe. It is nothing worked up, but it comes from the heart. "With the heart man believeth unto righteousness; and with the mouth, confession is made unto salvation." So when the Holy Ghost life comes in, the mouth opens, through the power of the Spirit in the heart. Glory to God!

"There were, dwelling at Jerusalem, Jews, devout men, out of every nation under heaven. Now when this was noised abroad, the multitude came together, and were confounded, because that every man heard them speak in his own language. And they were all amazed and marveled, saying one to another, 'Behold, are not all these which speak, Galileans. And how hear we every man speak in our own tongue wherein we were born?" Acts. 2:5-8.

Beloved, if you do not know the language that you speak, do not puzzle yourself about it, for the Lord did not promise us He would tell us what language we were speaking, but He promised us the interpretation of what we speak.

In seeking the baptism, first get a clear, definite witness in your soul that you have the abiding Christ within. Then there will be no trouble in receiving the Pentecostal baptism, through faith in our Lord and Savior, Jesus Christ, for it is a free gift that comes without repentance. Bless His holy name!

The Holy Spirit Bishop of the Church

It is the office work of the Holy Spirit to preside over the entire work of God on earth. —John 10:3 Jesus was our Bishop, while on earth, but now He has sent the Holy Ghost, Amen, to take His place, not men. —John 14:16; 15:26; 16:7-14. Praise His holy name!

The Holy Ghost is to infuse with divine power, and to invest with heavenly authority. No religious assembly is legal without His presence and His transaction. We should recognize Him as the Teacher of teachers.

The reason why there are so many of God's people without divine power today without experimental salvation, wrought out in their hearts by the Blood, by the power of the blessed Holy Spirit, is because they have not accepted Him as their Teacher, as their Leader, as their Comforter. Jesus said in His precious Word that if He went away He would send us another Comforter. The need of men and women today in their lives, is a Comforter, Praise our God! We have received this blessed Comforter, and it is heaven in our souls. We can sing with all our hearts:

> "What matter where on earth we dwell,
> On mountain top, or in the dell,
> In cottage or a mansion fair,
> Where Jesus is, 'tis heaven there."

Bless His holy name! May God help every one of His Blood bought children to receive this blessed Comforter. Glory to His name!

Hallelujah! Hosannah to His omnipotent name! Oh, He is reigning in my soul! Hallelujah! I just feel like the song which says:

"Oh, spread the tidings round
Wherever man is found,
Wherever human hearts
And human woes abound,
Let every Christian tongue
Proclaim the joyful sound,
The Comforter has come!

Many people today think we need new churches, (that is to say church buildings,) stone structures, brick structures, modern improvements, new choirs, trained singers right from the conservatories, paying from seven to fifteen hundred dollars a year for singing, fine pews, fine chandeliers, everything that could attract the human heart to win souls to the meeting house is used in this twentieth century. We find that they have reached the climax, but all of that has failed to bring divine power and salvation to precious souls. Sinners have gone to the meeting house, heard a nice, fine, eloquent oration on Jesus, or on some particular church, or on some noted man.

The people have been made glad to go because they have seen great wealth, they have seen people in the very latest styles, in different costumes, and loaded down with jewelry, decorated from head to foot with diamonds, gold and silver. The music in the church has been sweet, and it is found that a good many of the church people seem to be full of love, but there has always been a lack of power. We wonder why sinners are not being converted, and why it is that the church is always making improvements, and failing to do the work that Christ called her to do.

It is because men have taken the place of Christ and the Holy Spirit.

The church had the right idea that we need bishops and elders, but they must be given authority by our Lord and Savior Jesus Christ, and their qualifications for these offices must be the enduement of the power of the Holy Ghost. Jesus, after choosing His disciples, said, in John 15:16 "Ye have not chosen me, but I have chosen you and ordained you, that ye should go and bring forth fruit, and that your fruit should remain, that whatsoever ye shall ask of the Father, in my name, He may give it you." Praise our God! The Lord Jesus ordained His disciples with His own blessed hands, before going back to glory, but He put the credentials in their hearts on the day of Pentecost, when they were baptized with the Holy Ghost and fire. Hallelujah!

This was the authority that made them His witnesses unto the uttermost parts of the earth, for without the blessed Holy Spirit, in all of His fullness, we are not able to witness unto the uttermost parts of the earth. We must be coworkers with Him, partakers of the Holy Ghost. Then, when He is in us, in all of His fullness, He will manifest Himself. Signs and miracles will follow. This is the office work of the Holy Spirit in the churches. Amen.

I pray God that all Christ's people and ministers everywhere will please stop by the headquarters, the Jerusalem before God, for their credentials. Then they are entitled to receive credentials from the visible church. But the main credential is to be baptized with the Holy Ghost. Instead of new preachers from the theological schools and academies, the same old preachers, baptized with the Holy Ghost and fire, the same old deacons, the same old plain church buildings will do.

When the Holy Ghost comes in He will cleanse out dead forms and ceremonies, and will give life and power to His ministers and preachers, in the same old church buildings. But without the Holy Ghost they are simply tombstones.

We must always recognize that a meeting house is simply a place, where Christ's people gather to worship, and not the church. The church is planted in our hearts, through the Blood of Jesus Christ, for Christ said in Matthew 16:16, "Upon this rock will I build my church, and the gates of hell shall not prevail against it." We see, if these meeting houses and such buildings were really churches of Christ, the storms, cyclones, and fire could not harm them; but we see them blown down by storms and burned down. But, through the precious Blood of Christ, this church that He plants in our souls will stand throughout eternity.

The first thing in every assembly is to see that He, the Holy Ghost, is installed as the chairman. The reason why we have so many dried up missions and churches today, is because they have not the Holy Ghost as the chairman. They have some man in His place. Man is all right in his place, that is when he is filled with the power of the Holy Ghost, for it is not man that does the work, but the Holy Ghost from the glory land, sent by Jesus to work through this tabernacle of clay. Wherever you find the Holy Ghost as the chairman in any assembly, you will find a fruitful assembly, you will find children being born unto God.
Just as it takes a father and a mother to bring forth children of this natural life, so it takes the Word and the Spirit to bring forth children of the spiritual birth. There must be a father and there must be a mother. God chooses human instruments to preach the Word unto the people, and the Holy Ghost gives birth to everyone who receives the Word of Christ, which means the new birth. Praise our God. Where a Holy Ghost man preaches the Word of God, the Lord will bring forth sons and daughters unto his administration.

Jesus Christ is the archbishop of these assemblies, and He must be recognized. Also we must recognize the Holy Spirit in all of His office work. He takes the members into the church, which is the body of Christ. Through repentance to God, and faith in Jesus, they become the members of the church of Christ. And they remain members as long as they live free from sin. When they commence sinning, the Holy Ghost, the chairman and bishop, the presiding elder, turns them out, and they know when they are turned out of this church. They don't have to go and ask their pastor or their preacher, for they feel within their own soul that the glory has left them—the joy, the peace, the rest and comfort. Then when they feel the lack in their souls, if they will confess their sins, God, the Holy Ghost, will accept them back into the church.

Oh, thank God for this holy way. I am so glad that sham battles are over. Men and women must live straight, holy, pure lives, free from sin, or else they have no part with Christ Jesus. When men and women are filled with the Holy Ghost, everywhere they go, living waters will flow.

The Lord promised that out of our innermost being living rivers of water should flow. This is the Holy Ghost. Amen! The mighty Pison, the Gihon, the Hiddekel, the Euphrates of our soul will flow, representing the rivers of salvation. Amen!

The Marriage Tie

Marriage is a divine institution which God Himself has instituted. Gen. 2:18, 24. "And the Lord God said, It is not good that man should be alone; I will make him an help meet for him. Therefore shall a man leave his father and his mother and shall cleave unto his wife; and they twain shall be one flesh." 1Cor. 11:9. "Neither was the man created for the woman, but the woman for the man."

God commended it. Gen. 2:18 and Prov. 18:22. "Whoso findeth a wife findeth a good thing, and obtaineth favor of the Lord."

God is in it. Matt. 19:4, 6. "And He answered and said unto them, Have ye not read that He which made them at the beginning made them male and female. Wherefore they are no more twain but one flesh. What therefore God hath joined together let not man put asunder."

It is honorable in all. Heb. 13:4. "Marriage is honorable in all and the bed undefiled, but whoremongers and adulterers God will judge." Christ attended a wedding in Canaan. He went to adorn it, to beautify it with His presence. John 2:1,2. "And the third day there was a marriage in Cana of Galilee, and the mother of Jesus was there. And both Jesus was called and His disciples to the marriage."

The forbidding to marry is the doctrine of devils. 1Tim. 4:1,3. "Now the Spirit speaketh expressly that in the latter times some shall depart from the faith, giving heed to seducing spirits and doctrines of devils; and forbidding to marry."

Marriage Binding for Life

God has approved of but one wife and one husband. Gen. 2:24. "Therefore shall a man leave his father and his mother, and shall cleave unto his wife; and they twain shall be one flesh." Matt. 19:3-6. "The Pharisees also came unto Him tempting Him, and saying unto Him, Is it lawful for a man to put away his wife for every cause? And He answered and said unto them, Have ye not read that He which made them at the beginning made them male and female, and said, For this cause shall a man leave father and mother, and shall cleave to his wife; and they twain shall be one flesh? Wherefore they are no more twain but one flesh. What therefore God hath joined together, let not man put asunder."

The husband and wife are bound together for life. Rom. 7:2. "For the woman which hath an husband is bound by the law to her husband so long as he liveth; but if the husband is dead, she is loosed from the law of her husband." 1 Cor. 7:39. The wife is bound by the law as long as her husband liveth; but if her husband be dead, she is at liberty to be married to whom she will, only in the Lord."

No court of man should sever the marriage tie. Matt. 19:6. "Wherefore they are no more twain but one flesh. What therefore God hath joined together let not man put asunder." Death alone severs the marriage tie. Heb. 13:4.

Moses' Law of Divorce

Under Moses' law, he suffered men to divorce their wives and marry again, because of the hardness of their hearts Matt. 19:7,8. "They say unto Him, Why did Moses then command to give a writing of divorcement, and to put her away? He saith unto them, Moses, because of the hardness of your hearts suffered you to put away your wives; but from the beginning it was not so." Under Moses' law they had been accustomed, for any uncleanness, adultery, fornication or some cause not as much as that, to put away the wife by giving her a bill of divorcement, and she could go and be another man's wife. But under the New Testament law, the law of Christ, she is bound by the law to her husband till death.

The Edenic Standard of Matrimony

Jesus did away with the divorce law, and restored matrimony back to the Edenic standard. Under Moses' law the sacredness of matrimony was lost through the hardness of hearts. But under the law of grace, it is restored back as in the beginning of grace. Praise God. God's promises are true and sure. Hallelujah! Amen.

Under the New Testament law, the law of Christ, there is but one cause for which a man may put away his wife, but no right to marry again. This cause is fornication or adultery. Matt. 5:31,32. "It hath been said, Whosoever shall put away his wife, let him give her a writing of divorcement; but I say unto you that whosoever shall put away his wife, saving for the cause of fornication, causeth her to commit adultery; and whosoever shall marry her that is divorced committeth adultery." Matt. 19:9. "And I say unto you, Whosoever shall put away his wife, except it be for fornication, and shall marry another committeth adultery; and whosoever marrieth her which is put away doth commit adultery." These two scriptures are just the same in meaning. Matt. 5: 31, 32 is the key to the whole subject. It settles the question.

Forbidden to Marry Again

After a man has lawfully put away his wife, or a wife has lawfully put away her husband, they are positively forbidden to marry again, under the New Testament law, until the former companion is dead. Mark 10:11, 12. "And He saith unto them, Whosoever shall put away his wife, and marry another, committeth adultery against her. And if a woman shall put away her husband, and be married to another, she committeth adultery." Luke 16:18. "Whosoever putteth away his wife and marrieth another, committeth adultery; and whosoever marrieth her that is put away from her husband committeth adultery." Rom. 7:2,3. "For the woman which hath an husband is bound by the law to her husband so long as he liveth; but if the husband be dead, she is loosed from the law of her husband. So then if while her husband liveth, she be married to another man, she shall be called an adulteress; but if her husband be dead, she is free from that law; so that she is no adulteress though she be married to another man."

Adultery and Fornication

The act of adultery is between a married person and another who is not the lawful companion. Both parties may be married or only one. When only one is married, the act is called fornication. Matt. 19:9 and 5:32. Jesus said, "Whosoever shall put away his wife, saving for the cause of fornication causeth her to commit adultery." These sins are just the same, only one is committed while living with a husband and the other is when one has separated and married again.

No man can enter the kingdom of heaven without confessing and forsaking adultery and fornication. Gal. 5:19,21, "Now the works of the flesh are manifest which are these, adultery, fornication, uncleanness, lasciviousness, envyings, murders, drunkenness, revelings, and such like; of the which I tell you before, as I have also told you in time past, that they which do such things shall not inherit the kingdom of God." Isa. 55:7, "Let the wicked forsake his way and the unrighteous man his thoughts; and let him return unto the Lord, and he will have mercy upon him; and to our God for He will abundantly pardon."

The Innocent Party

If Jesus had intended that the innocent party should marry, He would have said so, and would not have said, Moses suffered it because of the hardness of your hearts. Jesus makes it very plain. If the innocent party marries, they are living in adultery. Jesus is showing the sacredness of matrimony. Dear beloved, let us obey God in spite of everything. There is one Scripture where many people are tied up, it is Matt. 19:9, where Jesus said, "But I say unto you that whosoever shall put away his wife, except for the cause of fornication, and shall marry another committeth adultery, and whosoever marrieth her that is put away committeth adultery." Now dear loved ones, let us stop and pray over this. "Except it be for fornication and marrieth another." Some think that this party would be entitled to marry again, but let us stop and see what Jesus is teaching here. If he puts away his wife except for the cause of fornication, he committeth a sin, because he will cause her to commit adultery. Therefore he is bound by the law as long as she lives, bound right to the Edenic standard. Amen.

Dear loved ones, if Jesus had instituted that the innocent party could get another wife, He would be instituting the same thing that was permitted by Moses, and would have the church filled with that today.

Now the reason Jesus gave him permission to put away his wife for the cause of fornication was that she is already adulterous, so her adultery gave him a lawful right to separate. While it gives him that right, yet it does not give him the right to get another wife while she lives.

Paul in 1 Tim. 3:2 says, "A bishop then must be blameless, the husband of one wife. He also says, 1 Tim. 5:9, "Let not a widow be taken into the number under threescore years old, having been the wife of one man." This shows plainly that they recognized in the church that a man was to have one wife and a woman one husband.

After Light Has Come

Rom. 7:2, 3 and 1 Cor. 7:39 give us very clear light. O may God help us to accept Bible salvation, instead of having our opinion and losing our souls. Dear beloved, you that have two wives or two husbands, before you had light on it, you lived that way and had no condemnation. God did not condemn you until you received the light upon His Word on this subject; but now God holds you responsible for the light. If you continue in the old life after light has come upon you, then you will be in the sight of God an adulterer or an adulteress, and you are bound to lose your experience or substitute something in the place of what God hath wrought. "If we walk in the light as He is in the light we have fellowship one with another and the Blood of Jesus Christ His Son cleanseth us from all sin." Let us obey God's Word if it takes our right eye or right hand.

So we find under the New Testament there is no putting away the first wife and getting another. Death is the only thing that severs the marriage tie. Rom. 7:2 and 1 Cor. 7: 39

Letter to one seeking the Holy Ghost

Dear Beloved in Christ Jesus:

The Lord Jesus has said in His precious Word, "Blessed are they which do hunger and thirst after righteousness, for they shall be filled." Matt. 5:6. God's promises are true and sure. We can rest upon His promises. He says, "Blessed are the pure in heart, for they shall see God. Matt. 5:8. "Blessed are the poor in spirit, for theirs is the kingdom of heaven." Matt. 5: 3.

The Lord Jesus is always ready to fill the hungry, thirsty soul, for He said in His precious Word, "He that believeth on Me as the scripture hath said, out of his innermost being shall flow rivers of living water.

(But this spoke He of the Spirit which they that believe on Him should receive: for the Holy Ghost was not yet given; because that Jesus was not yet glorified.)" John 7: 38, 39. But, praise God, He is given to us today.

All we have to do it to obey the first chapter of Acts, and wait for the promise of the Father upon our souls. The Lord Jesus said in His precious Word. "Behold I send the promise of My Father upon you; but tarry ye in the city of Jerusalem until ye be endued with power from on high. (Luke 24, 49.) For John truly baptized with water; but ye shall be baptized with the Holy Ghost not many days hence. "Ye shall receive power after that the Holy Ghost is come upon you; and ye shall be witnesses unto Me both in Jerusalem and in all Judea, and in Samaria and unto the uttermost part of the earth." Acts 1:5, 8. They tarried until they received the mighty power of the baptism with the Holy Spirit upon their souls. Then God put the credentials in their hearts, and put the ring of authority on their finger, and sealed them in the forehead with the Father's name, and wrote on their heart the name of the New Jerusalem, and put in their hand the stone with the name written that no man knoweth save he that receiveth it. Praise the Lord, for His mercy endureth forever. Let us stand upon His promises. They are sure, they will not break.

The Lord Jesus says, "Behold, I give you power to tread on serpents and scorpions, and over all the power of the enemy; and nothing shall by any means hurt you." Luke 10:19. Dear loved one, the Lord Jesus when He rose from the dead said, "All power is given unto Me in heaven and in earth. Go ye therefore, and teach all nations, baptizing them in the name of the Father, and of the Son, and of the Holy Ghost. (Matt. 28:19) He that believeth and is baptized shall be saved; but he that believeth not shall be damned. And these signs shall follow them that believe; in My name shall they cast out devils; they shall speak with new tongues; they shall take up serpents; and if they drink any deadly thing, it shall not hurt them; they shall lay hands on the sick and they shall recover." Mark 16:16-18. And they went forth and preached everywhere, the Lord working with them, and confirming the Word with signs following. Praise His dear name, for He is just the same today.

The first thing in order to receive this precious and wonderful baptism with the Holy Spirit, we want to have a clear knowledge of justification by faith according to the Bible. Rom. 5:1, "Therefore being justified by faith, we have peace with God through our Lord Jesus Christ," faith that all our actual sins may be washed away. Actual sin means committed sin.

And then the second step is to have a real knowledge of sanctification, which frees us from original sin—the sin that we were born with, which we inherited from our father Adam. We were not responsible for that sin until we received light, for we could not repent of a sin that we did not commit. When we came to the Lord as a sinner, we repented to God of our actual sins, and God for Christ's sake pardoned us and washed our sin and pollution away, and planted eternal life in our souls. Afterwards we saw in the Word of God, "This is the will of God, even your sanctification." 1Thess. 4:3, also John 17:15-19. We consecrated ourselves to God, and the Lord Jesus sanctified our souls, and made us every whit clean.

Then after we were clearly sanctified, we prayed to God for the baptism with the Holy Spirit. So He sent the Holy Spirit to our hearts and filled us with His blessed Spirit, and He gave us the Bible evidence, according to the 2nd chapter of Acts verses 1 to 4, speaking with other tongues as the Spirit gives utterance.

Praise our God; He is the same yesterday, today, and forever. Receive Him just now and He will fill you. Amen. Don't get discouraged but pray until you are filled, for the Lord says, "Men ought always to pray and not to faint." Don't stop because you do not receive the baptism with the Holy Ghost at the first, but continue until you are filled. The Lord Jesus told His disciples to tarry until they were endued with power from on high. Many people today are willing to tarry just so long, and then they give up and fail to receive their personal Pentecost that would measure with the Bible. The Lord Jesus says, "Ye shall be filled." He says that to the person that hungers and thirsts after righteousness and He says they are blessed. So if there is a hunger and thirst in our souls for righteousness, we are blest of Him. Praise His dear name!

Christ's Messages to the Church

The last message given to the church was by the Holy Ghost, from our Lord and Saviour Jesus Christ through Brother John on the Isle of Patmos. Dear beloved, we read in Revelations 1:5-7, these words, "Unto Him that loved us and washed us from our sins in His own Blood." Hallelujah to His name. "And hath made us kings and priests unto God and the Father; to Him be glory and dominion for ever and ever. Amen. Behold He cometh with clouds; and every eye shall see Him, and they also which pierced Him; and all kindreds of the earth shall wail because of Him. Even so, Amen."

This is the beginning of this wonderful and blessed message given to our beloved Apostle John while he was suffering for the word of God and for the testimony of Jesus Christ. Jesus knew all about His servant, though He had been living in Heaven more than half a century after His ascension. And He came and visited that beloved apostle, the disciple who loved Jesus and leaned on His bosom. He now was old but had been faithful to the trust that Jesus had given him. He had passed through awful trials and tribulations for this precious Gospel, even being boiled in a caldron of oil, tradition tells us; but, blessed be God, they were not able to kill him. And when they got tired of this precious Holy Ghost Gospel messenger, preaching to them the faith of Jesus, they banished him to the Isle of Patmos. And while he was in the Spirit on the Lord's day, our blessed Jesus Christ, the Son of the living

God, our great Redeemer, came and gave him this wonderful revelation, and introduced Himself to John as, "I am Alpha and Omega, the beginning and the ending, said the Lord, which is, and which was, and which is to come, the Almighty." Hallelujah.

O beloved, the Lord Jesus knows all about our trials and tribulations, because He was a man of sorrows and acquainted with grief. His whole life was a life of suffering. We read in Heb. 5:7, 8, "Though He were a son, yet learned He obedience by the things which He suffered. And being made perfect, He became the author of eternal salvation unto all them that obey." O bless our God. Just to think that Jesus was God's Son, and all things were made by Him and for Him; yet He was foreordained before the foundation of the world that He should die.

He was slain before the foundation of the world. So the Word of God became flesh and dwelt among men and was handled by men, and lived in this world. And at the age of 33 years, He paid the debt on Calvary's cross. O beloved, if we expect to reign with Him, we must suffer with Him—not that people must be sick or unhealthy or go with a long face, but we must bear all things and keep the faith of Jesus in our hearts. Our lives now are with the suffering Christ: and "it doth not yet appear what we shall be, but we know that when He shall appear, we shall be like Him; for we shall see Him as He is." Glory to Jesus.

After Jesus introduced Himself, He gave John these blessed messages to the church. John was permitted to see from the beginning of the church age on down to the white throne judgment, the final winding up of the world. He was permitted to see the overcomers. He was permitted to see the millennial reign with Jesus in triumph over the kingdoms of Satan; to see this old world pass away, to see the new heavens and new earth, and the New Jerusalem coming down from God out of Heaven. John saw things past, things present, and things in the future. He had witnessed the glory and power of the apostolic church, and saw the falling away of the church, and God sent him to the church with this blessed message; that she should come back to her first love.

The Vision of Jesus in His Church

The most striking passage of Scripture in the first chapter is where John was permitted to see Jesus walking among the golden candlesticks, which represent the church. Christ is in His church today to fill men and women, to heal their bodies, save and sanctify their souls, and to put His finger upon every wrong and mean thing in the church. His rebuke is against it, for He hates sin today as much as He ever did when He walked by the Sea of Galilee. Glory to His name. Jesus hates impure doctrine just as much as when He rebuked the Pharisees for their impure doctrine.

John beheld Jesus in His glorified body. What a holy scene it was: the Son of God clothed with a garment down to the foot and girt about the paps with a golden girdle. "His head and His hairs were white like wool, as white as snow." Hallelujah. There is nothing but purity and holiness in our Saviour. And "His eyes were as a flame of fire." Glory to Jesus. "And His feet like to fine brass, as if they burned in a furnace. And His voice as the sound of many waters," which represents many people. Bless God.

"And He had in His right hand seven stars." This represents His Holy Ghost ministers. Jesus has them in His hand, that is to say that He gave them the authority to preach the Gospel and power over devils. All of our authority and power comes from Jesus. It is so sweet when we know that we have authority from Jesus. Bless His holy name. O beloved, when we know Jesus Christ has His minister in His hand, we know that minister is a live preacher. Glory to Jesus. Hallelujah. A live minister represents one that is saved, sanctified and filled with the Holy Spirit. Then the same life, the same authority that Jesus promised we will find in his life.

"And out of His mouth went a sharp two-edged sword, and His countenance was as the sun shineth in His strength." The glory of God shining through the blessed Christ. "And when I saw Him, I fell at His feet as one dead. And He laid His right hand upon me, saying unto me, Fear not; I am the first and the last." Praise God, Jesus is alive and because He lives everyone that gets Christ is alive in the blessed Holy Spirit. The Blood of Jesus Christ does give life, power and fire, joy, peace, happiness and faith. Hallelujah to His name.

"I am He that liveth and was dead, and behold, I am alive for evermore." Bless His holy name. He wanted John to know that He was the same One that hung and bled and died and shed His precious Blood on Calvary's cross, went down into the grave, and rose again.

This ought to make the whole body of Christ's people everywhere happy to know that Jesus is alive for evermore. Hallelujah to His name. Then He said, "And have the keys of hell and of death." Bless God. No wonder Bro. David said, "Though I walk through the valley of the shadow of death, I will fear no evil, for Thou art with me." When we get Jesus Christ in our hearts, we can use the word and it is a comfort to us to know that we have passed from death to life.

Then He told John particularly, "Write these things which thou hast seen, and the things which are, and the things which shall be hereafter."

The Message to the Church of Ephesus

Then He gave him the messages to the seven churches. "And to the angel of the church at Ephesus write, "These things saith He that holdeth the seven stars in His right hand, who walketh in the midst of the seven golden candlesticks."

Hallelujah to His name. Ephesus was a city of Asia, quite a commercial city, a city of wealth, refinement, culture and great learning. It was where John preached and where Paul had labored. Many people there had been saved and baptized with the Spirit. Paul had witnessed a great scene in Ephesus where he had preached the Gospel of the Son of God and of the doctrine of the baptism with the Holy Spirit, and 12 men after hearing of this blessed doctrine, received water baptism, and when Paul laid his hands on them, they received the baptism with the Holy Ghost and spoke with tongues and prophesied. Acts.19:6. So Ephesus was a favored place, but the message was sent to it and to all the churches of Asia.

This is a true picture of the Lord Jesus' eyes upon the church ever since its beginning, and will be unto the end. We are living near the close of the Gentile age down in the Laodicean period, when the church has become as formal as the Laodiceans. This message was first to the church of Ephesus.

I Know Thy Works

The Lord Jesus said, "I know thy works." God knows our works, He knows our hearts. "And thy labor and thy patience, and how thou canst not bear them which are evil; and thou has tried them which say they are apostles, and are not, and hast found them liars; and hast borne and hast patience, and for My name's sake hast labored and hast not fainted." Bless our God. That is more than many churches today could receive from the Master. Jesus commended them for what they had done. He commended them for their faithfulness. He is not like men.

He knows our hearts, our trials, our conditions. But bless God, He does not make any allowance for sin. He hates sin today as much as He ever did. Yet He does not come to destroy us or condemn us, but to seek and to save us.

"Nevertheless I have somewhat against thee, because thou hast left thy first love." The Lord does not want anything to get between us and Him. O may every precious child in these times that are getting the Holy Spirit not go into apostasy, but may they be a burning and a shining light for God, just as we were when we first received the baptism with the Holy Spirit. God wants us to keep the same anointing that we received and let nothing separate us from Christ.

Repentance

We find Jesus still preaches the same doctrine of repentance that He preached while on earth. In order to get right with God, He says, "Remember from whence thou art fallen and repent and do the first works, or else I will come unto thee quickly, and will remove thy candlestick out of his place, except thou repent." Dear beloved, if there is anything wrong in your life and Jesus has His finger upon it, O may you give it up, for Jesus is truly in His church today. This is the Holy Ghost dispensation and He does convince men of sin, righteousness and the judgment, and if we will be honest, God will bless us.

To the Church Today

When a church or mission finds that the power of God begins to leave, they should come as a whole and confess, and let all get down before God and repent and pray to God until the old time fire and power and love come back again. Many times the Holy Spirit will leave an assembly, mission or church because the pastor grieves Him, and sometimes not only the pastor but the whole body commences backbiting, whispering, tattling, or prejudice and partiality creep in, until the whole becomes corrupted and Jesus is just ready to spew them out of His mouth.

But, O beloved, let us then come to the 2nd chapter of Revelation and see what Jesus says to the assembly. He expects to find the church, when He comes back to earth again, just as full of fire and power and the signs following, as it was when He organized it on the day of Pentecost. Bless His holy name. May God help all His precious praying children to get back to the old Pentecostal power and fire and love. The church at that time was as terrible as an army with banners. She conquered every power of evil. Hypocrites were not able to remain in it any more than Ananias and Sapphira. God gave such wonderful love to His people.

Then He gave messages to every church, showing that Jesus' eyes are upon every church. His finger this day is upon every heart that does not measure to the fullness of holiness. God wants a holy church and all wrong cleansed away—fornication and adultery two wives, two husbands, not paying grocery bills, water bills, furniture bills, coal bills, gas bills, and all honest bills. God wants His people to be true and holy and He will work. Nothing can hinder. Bless His holy name.

I thank God for this wonderful message to the church, a message from heaven, given by Jesus to show that He is in the church, that He does walk among the golden candlesticks. He is in heaven, but through the power of the Holy Spirit, He walks in the church today. Nothing can be hidden from His pure eyes. He wants people to live the highest and deepest consecration to Him. He does not want their love for Him divided. Their first love is to Him.

Impure Doctrine

We find many of Christ's people tangled up in these days, committing spiritual fornication as well as physical fornication and adultery. They say, "Let us all come together; if we are not one in doctrine, we can be one in spirit." But, dear ones, we cannot all be one, except through the word of God. He says, "But this thou hast that thou hatest the deeds of the Nicolaitanes, which I also hate." I suppose that the apostolic church at Ephesus allowed people that were not teaching straight doctrine, not solid in the word of God, to remain in fellowship with them; and Jesus saw that a little leaven would leaven the whole, and His finger was right upon that impure doctrine. It had to be removed out of the church or He would remove the light and break the church up.

When we find things wrong, contrary to Scripture, I care not how dear it is, it must be removed. We cannot bring Agag among the children of Israel, for God says he must die. Saul saved Agag, which represented saving himself, the carnal nature or old man; but Samuel said Agag must die, and he drew his sword and slew him. Christ's precious word, which is the sword of Samuel, puts all carnality and sin to death. It means perfect obedience to walk with the Lord. There are many people in these last days that are not going to live a Bible salvation, they are going to take chances. But may God help everyone, if their right hand or right eye offend them to cast it from them. It is better to enter into life maimed, than for soul and body to be cast into hell fire.

The Lord says, "He that hath an ear, let him hear what the Spirit saith unto the churches; To him that overcometh will I give to eat of the tree of life which is in the midst of the paradise of God." O beloved, if we expect to reign with the Lord and Saviour Jesus Christ, we must overcome the world, the flesh, and the devil. There will be many that will be saved but will not be full overcomers to reign on this earth with our Lord. He will give us power to overcome if we are willing. Bless His holy name.

"To the Married"

1 Cor. 7.

In these days, so many deceptive spirits are in the world, that we have felt impressed by the blessed Holy Spirit to write a letter on the seventh chapter of First Corinthians, that blessed letter which Paul has sent to the church.

The Corinthian church was one of Paul's most gifted churches, and just as it is today, where a church is very gifted, the only safeguard from deceptive spirits is by rightly dividing the Word of God, to keep out fanaticism. We may let down on some lines and rise on others, but God wants everything to be balanced by the Word of God. Paul writing to Timothy (II Tim. 1:13, 14) says, "Hold fast the form of sound words which thou has heard of me, in faith and love which is in Christ Jesus. That good thing which was committed unto thee keep by the Holy Ghost which dwelleth in us." And again he says (II Tim. 3:14): "But continue thou in the things which thou hast learned and hast been assured of, knowing of whom thou hast learned them; and that from a child thou hast known the holy Scriptures, which are able to make thee wise unto salvation through faith which is in Christ Jesus.

All Scripture is given by inspiration of God, and is profitable for doctrine, for reproof, for correction, for instruction in righteousness: that the man of God may be perfect, thoroughly furnished unto all good works." So the Lord God wants us to search and compare scriptures with scriptures.

This Corinthian church had run into freeloveism, and a good many isms. Great division had arisen in it; it had split into several parts, and Paul had to settle them down into the Word of God. He writes this letter to them, for they had got into awful trouble.

Paul tells them in the first verse of this chapter to avoid immorality. He says, "Now concerning the things whereof ye wrote unto me, it is good for a man not to touch a woman." (He does not mean a married man here, he means a man that is single, as verses 8 and 26 show.) He says in the 7th verse, "Every man hath his proper gift of God." And to those that can receive this gift, Paul writes in verse 8, "I say therefore to the unmarried and widows, It is good for them if they abide even as I." That is to say, by living a single life, they would have more power in the Spirit. He writes this to the church, to any who are saved, sanctified and filled with the Holy Spirit. Paul thought it was best, but he showed that everyone had his proper gift of God. So he did not put any bondage upon the people of Christ, because he had no scripture for it.

He says in the second and third verses, "Nevertheless, to avoid fortification, let every man have his own wife, and let every woman have her own husband. Let the husband render unto the wife due benevolence: and likewise also the wife unto the husband." This of course means conjugal intercourse between man and wife. "The wife hath not power of her own body, but the husband: and likewise also the husband hath not power of his own body, but the wife." That is to say, that the husband has no authority to live separated, without the consent of his wife; and the wife has no authority of herself to live separated without the husband. Then he says in the 5th verse, "Defraud ye not one another, except it be with consent for a time, that ye may give yourselves to fasting and prayer; and come together again, that Satan tempt you not for your incontinency." That is to say that every wife and husband should abstain from impurity, and give themselves to fasting for a time. It should be by mutual agreement between the two to fast for power and blessing, and many times to avoid impurity. But he advised them to come again, "that Satan tempt you not for your incontinency." Paul here does not make this a law, but as one that had the Holy Spirit, he gives them this advice. He adds in the 6th verse, "But I speak this by permission and not of commandment." In Romans 1:26, 27, Paul shows there is a natural use for a wife, which is not lust. Speaking of the ungodly, he says, "For this cause God gave them up unto vile affections: for even their women did change the natural use into that which is against nature." May God help us to be clear teachers of His Word.

"I would that all men were even as I myself. But every man hath his proper gift of God, one after this manner and another after that." Paul is referring here to Matthew 19:12, where Jesus told the Pharisees that there were some men that were born eunuchs from their mother's womb (that is to say, unable to have wives), some have been made eunuchs of men (for other advantages in life) and there were some eunuchs for the kingdom of Heaven's sake. Men had prayed to God for this gift or blessing, just as Paul who said he wished all men were like him: he became no doubt a eunuch for the kingdom of Heaven's sake. Jesus Himself said (Matt. 19:11), "All men cannot receive this saying, save they to whom it is given." So Jesus did not put any bondage on men and women, but a man today that has received the power to become a eunuch for the kingdom of Heaven's sake can live a single life with all holiness and purity. Praise our God!

We must rightly divide the Scriptures and compare scripture with scripture so that there be no confusion and no deceptive spirit or wrong teaching may creep in.

Paul says in verses 29 to 31, "But this I say brethren, the time is short: it remaineth that both they that have wives be as though they had none; and they that weep as though they wept not; and they that rejoice as though they rejoiced not; and they that buy as though they possessed not; and they that use the world as not abusing it: for the fashion of this world passeth away." Bless the Lord! Now Paul in speaking this did not put any bondage on mothers to fear that they would not be able to meet Jesus in His coming, because they were bringing forth children.

Mothers and fathers that are saved and sanctified, to whom the Lord has given this gift of bringing forth children can live a pure and holy life before God and be of the bride of Christ, just as the bishop that teaches this holy Gospel can be the husband of one wife and raise his children in the fear of God.

Married couples who are mutually agreed, having received from the Lord power over both body, soul and spirit, God does not ask them to desire; but may they live as God has called them. Many times God gives this power to the husband before to the wife. Many times the wife has it; but in order to save the husband she has to submit to the husband. For God is not the author of confusion. This brings us back to the third verse of this same chapter. Also in Ephesians 5th chapter and 22nd verse, we read, "Wives, submit yourselves unto your husbands, as unto the Lord." Please read on down to the 33rd verse.

God does not make the husband the tyrant or cruel sovereign over the wife, neither does He make the wife to exercise tyranny over the husband, but He makes both one. God knows our hearts and our lives. Someone may ask what Jesus meant in Matt. 24:19, "And woe unto them that are with child, and to them that give suck in those days."

Well, beloved, here Jesus' heart was upon the people that would suffer in the awful tribulation that was coming to Jerusalem forty years after His ascension. He says to them, "But pray ye that your flight be not in the winter, neither on the Sabbath day." Jesus was the Son of God but He was a man of prayer. He asked His disciples to pray with Him in the Garden of Gethsemane. He knew that in the destruction of Jerusalem, if they prayed to God, the Father would not permit it to come to pass in the winter, neither on the Sabbath day. He knew if it was on the Sabbath day, the Jews would be keeping the old Mosaic law (Col. 2:16) "Of new moons and of Sabbath days, which were a shadow of things to come, but the body of Christ." (The greatest thing that people need in this day is Christ, and then all the days will come in their order and in their place.) Jesus knew if their flight occurred on the Sabbath day, all the gates of Jerusalem would be shut and the Christians could not get out, and the mothers could not escape; so His heart went out for the precious women. The Lord Jesus Christ knows all about our struggles. He knows all about our sufferings and our trials. He is touched with every infirmity and He remembers us. Bless His holy name.

May God help everyone that is getting saved to stay within the lids of God's word and wait on God, and He will make all things right. Now we can give up anything that we see is really of self-gratification. The Lord wants us to be temperate in all things. Bless His holy name. People that are desiring to get the victory over spirit, soul and body, can have it if they will trust God.

I have been asked so much on this question, and I can only give what God has revealed to me through His precious Word. Bless His holy name!

Sanctified on the Cross

"I pray not that Thou shouldst take them out of the world, but that Thou shouldst keep them from the evil. They are not of the world even as I am not of the world. Sanctify them through Thy truth, Thy word is truth." Jesus is still praying this prayer today for every believer to come and be sanctified. Glory to God! Sanctification makes us one with the Lord Jesus (Hebrews 2:11). Sanctification makes us holy as Jesus is.

Then the prayer of Jesus is answered, and we become one with Him, even as He is one with the Father. Bless His holy name.

He says again in 1 Thessalonians 4:3, For this is the will of God even your sanctification." It is His will fur every soul to be saved from all sin, actual and original. We get our actual sins cleansed away through the Blood of Jesus Christ at the Cross; hut our original sin we get cleansed on the Cross, it must be a real death to the old man. Romans 6:6, "Knowing this that our old man is crucified with Him, that the body of sin, might be destroyed, that henceforth we should not serve sin. For he that Is dead is freed from sin." It takes the death of the old man in order that Christ might be sanctified in us. It is not sufficient to have the old man stunned or knocked down, for he will rise again.

God is calling His people to true Holiness in these days. We thank God for the blessed light that He is giving us. He says in Ii Tim. 2:21: "Ifs man therefore purge himself from these. he shall be a vessel unto honor, sanctified and meet for the Master's use." He means for us to be purged from uncleanness and all kinds of sin. Then we shall be it vessel unto honor, sanctified and inset for the Master's use, and prepared unto every good work. Sanctification makes us holy and destroys the breed of sin, the love of sin and carnality. It makes us pure and whiter than snow. Bless His holy name!

The Lord Jesus says, "Blessed are the pure in heart." Sanctification makes us pure in heart. Any man that is saved and sanctified call feel the fire burning in his heart, when be calls on the name of Jesus. Oh, may God help men and women 'everywhere to lead a holy life, free from sin, for the Holy Spirit seeks to lead you out of sin into the marvelous light of the Sun of God.
The Word says. "Follow peace with all men and Holiness without which no man shall see the Lord." Therefore, beloved, when we get Jesus Christ our King of Peace in our hearts, we have the almighty Christ, the everlasting Father, the Prince of Peace. "Thou wilt keep him in perfect peace whose mind is stayed on Thee, because He trusteth in Thee." We shall have wisdom, righteousness and power. For God is righteous In all His ways and holy in all His arts. This Holiness means perfect love in our hearts, perfect love that casteth out fear.

Brother Paul says in order to become holy and live a holy life, we should abstain from all appearance of evil. Then the apostle adds, "And the very God of peace sanctify you wholly, and I pray God your whole spirit and soul and body he preserved blameless unto the coming of our Lord Jesus Christ" (1 Thessalonians 1: 22-23). "To the end He may establish your hearts unblameable in Holiness before God, even our Father, at the coming of our Lord Jesus Christ with all His saints." (ii Thessalonians 3:13). Bless His holy name. Oh, beloved, after you have received the light, it is Holiness or hell. God is calling for men and women in these days that will live a holy life free from sin. We should remain before God until His all cleansing Blood makes us holy, body, soul and spirit.

The Baptism of the Holy Ghost

The Azusa standard of the baptism with the Holy Ghost is according to the Bible in Acts 1:5,8; Acts 2:4 and Luke 24:49. Bless His holy name. Hallelujah to the Lamb for the baptism of the Holy Ghost and fire and speaking in tongues as the Spirit gives utterance.

Jesus gave the church at Pentecost the great lesson of how to carry on a revival, and it would be well for every church to follow Jesus' standard of the baptism of the Holy Ghost and fire.

"And when the day of Pentecost was fully come, they were all with one accord in one place." O beloved, there is where the secret is: one accord, one place, one heart, one soul, one mind, one prayer. If God can get a people anywhere in one accord and in one place, of one heart, mind, and soul, believing for this great power, it will fall and Pentecostal results will follow. Glory to God!

Apostolic Faith doctrine means one accord, one soul, one heart. May God help every child of His to live in Jesus' prayer: "That they all may be one, as Thou, Father, art in Me and I in Thee; that they all may be one in us; that the world may believe that Thou hast sent Me." Praise God! O how my heart cries out to God in these days that He would make every child of His see the necessity of living in the 17th chapter of John, that we may be one in the body of Christ, as Jesus has prayed. When we are sanctified through the truth, then we are one in Christ, and we can get into one accord for the gift or power of the Holy Ghost, and God will come in like a rushing mighty wind and fill every heart with the power of the Holy Spirit. Glory to His holy name. Bless God! O how I praise Him for this wonderful salvation that is spreading over this great earth. The baptism of the Holy Ghost brings the glory of God in our hearts.

The Holy Ghost Is Power

There is a great difference between a sanctified person and one that is baptized with the Holy Ghost and fire. A sanctified person is cleansed and filled with divine love, but the one that is baptized with the Holy Ghost has the power of God on his soul and has power with God and men, power over all the kingdoms of Satan and over all his emissaries. God can take a worm and thresh a mountain. Glory to God. Hallelujah!

In all Jesus' great revivals and miracles, the work was wrought by the power of the Holy Ghost flowing through His sanctified humanity.

When the Holy Ghost comes and takes us as His instruments, this is the power that convicts men and women and causes them to see that there is a reality in serving Jesus Christ. O beloved, we ought to thank God that He has made us the tabernacles of the Holy Ghost. When you have the Holy Ghost, you have an empire, a power within yourself.

Elijah was a power in himself through the Holy Ghost. He brought down fire from heaven. So when we get the power of the Holy Ghost, we will see the heavens open and the Holy Ghost power falling on earth, power over sickness, diseases and death.

The Lord never revoked the commission He gave to His disciples: "Heal the sick, cleanse the lepers, raise the dead," and He is going to perform these things if He can get a people in unity. The Holy Spirit is power with God and man. You have power with God as Elijah had.

God put man over all His works; but we know that when Adam sinned, he lost a great deal of his power; but now through the Blood of Jesus, He says, "Behold, I give you power to tread on serpents and scorpions, and over all the powers of the enemy." The Lord Jesus wants a church, when He comes back to earth, just like the one He started when He left the earth and organized it on the day of Pentecost.

Tarry in One Accord

O may every child of God seek his real personal Pentecost, stop quibbling and come to the standard that Jesus laid down for us in Acts 2: "And suddenly there came a sound from heaven as of a rushing mighty wind, and It filled all the house where they were sitting."

Glory to God! O beloved, if you wait on God for this baptism of the Holy Ghost just now, and can get two or three people together that are sanctified through the Blood of Christ, and all get into one accord, God will send the baptism of the Holy Ghost upon your souls as the rain falls from heaven. You may not have a preacher to come to you and preach the doctrine of the Holy Ghost and fire, but you can obey Jesus' saying in the passage. "Where two or three are gathered together in My name, there am I in the midst of them."

This is Jesus' baptism: and if two or three are gathered together in His name and pray for the baptism of the Holy Ghost, they can have it this day or this night, because it is the promise of the Father. Glory to God!

This was the Spirit that filled the house as a rushing mighty wind. The Holy Ghost is typified by wind, air, breath, life, fire. "And there appeared unto them cloven tongues like as of fire, and it sat upon each of them; and they were all filled with the Holy Ghost and began to speak with other tongues as the Spirit gave them utterance."

So, beloved, when you get your personal Pentecost, the signs will follow in speaking with tongues as the Spirit gives utterance. This is true. Wait on God and you will find it a truth in your own life. God's promises are true and sure.

The Baptism Falls on a Clean Heart

Jesus is our example. "And Jesus being full of the Holy Ghost, returned from Jordan, and was led by the Spirit." We find in reading the Bible that the baptism with the Holy Ghost and fire falls on a clean, sanctified life, for we see according to the Scriptures that Jesus was "holy, harmless, undefiled," and filled with wisdom and favor with God and man, before God anointed Him with the Holy Ghost and power.

For in Luke 2:40 we read. "Jesus waxed strong in spirit, filled with wisdom, and the grace of God was upon Him"; and in Luke 2:52, "And Jesus increased in wisdom and stature, and in favor with God and man."

After Jesus was empowered with the Holy Ghost at Jordan, He returned in the power of the Spirit into Galilee, and there went out a fame of Him through all the region round about." Glory to God! He was not any more holy or any more meek, but had greater authority. "And He taught in their synagogues, being glorified of all."

Beloved, if Jesus who was God Himself, needed the Holy Ghost to empower Him for His ministry and His miracles, how much more do we children need the Holy Ghost baptism today. O that men and women would tarry for the baptism with the Holy Ghost and fire upon their souls, that the glory may be seen upon them just as it was upon the disciples on the day of Pentecost in the fiery emblem of tongues.

The tongues of fire represented the great Shekina glory. So today the Shekina glory rests day and night upon those who are baptized with the Holy Ghost, while He abides in their souls. For His presence is with us.

Glory to His name. I thank Him for this wonderful salvation. Let us ring His praises through all the world that all men may know that the Comforter has come. Bless His dear name!

Jesus' First Sermon after His Baptism

"And He came to Nazareth where He was brought up; and as His custom was, He went into the synagogue on the Sabbath day and stood up for to read. And there was delivered unto Him the book of the prophet Esaias. And when He had opened the book, He found the place where it is written: The Spirit of the Lord is upon Me because He hath anointed Me to preach the Gospel to the poor: He hath sent me to heal the broken-hearted, to preach deliverance to the captives, and recovering of sight to the blind, to set at liberty them that are bruised, to preach the acceptable year of the Lord." (Luke 4:18, 19.) Hallelujah.

Glory to God! This is Jesus' sermon after His baptism with the Holy Ghost, preaching in the synagogue. He acknowledged that the Spirit of God was upon Him.

Jesus was the Son of God and born of the Holy Ghost and filled with the Holy Ghost from His mother's womb: but the baptism of the Holy Ghost came upon His sanctified humanity at the Jordan. In His humanity, He needed the Third Person of the Trinity to do His work. And He could truly say that His fingers became instruments of the Holy Ghost to cast out devils.

The Holy Ghost Flows through Pure Channels

If men and women today will consecrate themselves to God, and get their hands and feet and eyes and affections, body and soul, all sanctified, how the Holy Ghost will use such people. He will find pure channels to flow through sanctified avenues for His power. People will be saved, sanctified, healed and baptized with the Holy Ghost and fire.

The baptism of the Holy Ghost comes through our Lord and Savior Jesus Christ by faith in His word. In order to receive it, we must first be sanctified. Then we can become His witnesses unto the uttermost parts of the earth. You will never have an experience to measure with Acts 2:4 and 16, 17, until you get your personal Pentecost or the baptism with the Holy Ghost and fire. (Matt 3:11)

This is the latter rain that God is pouring out upon His humble children in the last days. We are preaching a Gospel that measures with the great commission that Jesus gave His disciples on the day when He arose from the dead. (Matt. 28:19,20) "Go ye therefore and teach all nations, baptizing them in the name of the Father, and of the Son, and of the Holy Ghost: teaching them to observe all things whatsoever I have commanded you: and lo, I am with you alway, even unto the end of the world. Amen!" They received the power to measure with this commission on the day of Pentecost. (Acts 2:4.) Bless the lord. O how I bless God to see His mighty power manifested in these last days. God wants His people to receive the baptism with the Holy Ghost and fire.

The Pentecostal power, when you sum it all up, is just more of God's love. If it does not bring more love, it is simply a counterfeit. Pentecost means to live right in the 13th chapter of First Corinthians, which is the standard. When you live there, you have no trouble to keep salvation. This is Bible religion. It is not a manufactured religion.

Pentecost makes us love Jesus more and love our brothers more. It brings us all into one common family.

The Holy Ghost and the Bride

We read in Rev., 22:17, "The Spirit and the bride say come." O how sweet it is for us to have this blessed privilege of being a co-worker with the Holy Ghost. He inspires us with faith in God's word and endues us with power for service for the Master. Bless His dear name! Every man and woman that receives the baptism of the Holy Ghost is the bride of Christ. They have a missionary spirit for saving souls. They have the spirit of Pentecost. Glory to God!

"And let him that heareth say, come, and let him that is athirst, come; and whosoever will, let him take the water of life freely." O what a blessed text. The bride of Christ is calling the thirsty to come to Jesus, because this is the work of the Holy Ghost in the believer. He intercedes for the lost; He groans for them.

The Spirit also calls the believer to come to Jesus and get sanctified. He points the sanctified to Jesus for his baptism with the Holy Ghost. When you are baptized with the Holy Ghost, you will have power to call sinners to Jesus, and they will be saved, and sanctified, and baptized with the Holy Ghost and fire. Amen!

Christ's bride is pure and spotless. "Thou art all fair, my love, there is no spot in thee." (Sol. Songs. 4:7.) Christ's bride is clean, free from sin and all impurity. He gave Himself for her, that He might sanctify and cleanse the church with the washing of water by the word. That He might present it to Himself a glorious church, not having spot or wrinkle or any such thing, but that it should be holy and without blemish. (Eph., 5:25,27).

Christ's bride has but one husband. (2 Cor., 11:2.) She is subject to Him. (Eph., 5:25.) The Bridegroom is the Son of God. (2 Cor., 11:2.)

We are married to Christ now in the Spirit. (Rom., 7:2,4.) Not only when He comes are we married to Christ but right now, if you are sanctified and baptized with the Holy Ghost and fire, you are married to Him already. God has a people to measure up to the Bible standard in this great salvation. Bless His holy name. Amen!

Made in the USA
Monee, IL
18 May 2021